IMAGES
of America

CLINTON
1940–1980

Dr. E. R. Pinson, Dr. William W. Stevens, Charles A. Tidwell, Dr. Joe Cooper, Dr. Norman O'Neal, and E. L. Douglas stand on the campus of Mississippi College in front of the Provine Chapel. (Courtesy of Mississippi College.)

ON THE COVER: The Mississippi College Choctaw Band marches down College Street toward campus. (Courtesy of Robert Wall.)

IMAGES
of America

CLINTON
1940–1980

Chad Chisholm

ARCADIA
PUBLISHING

Published by Arcadia Publishing
Charleston SC, Chicago IL, Portsmouth NH, San Francisco CA

Library of Congress Catalog Card Number: 2007939870

For all general information contact Arcadia Publishing at:
Telephone 843-853-2070
Fax 843-853-0044
E-mail sales@arcadiapublishing.com
For customer service and orders:
Toll-Free 1-888-313-2665

Visit us on the Internet at www.arcadiapublishing.com

For Emily

CONTENTS

ACKNOWLEDGMENTS

This author owes many thanks to the Clinton Visitor Center staff and its director, Jacque McLemore. Jacque's efforts these past two years have been indelible, more than can ever be expressed in words. I am grateful to Kristi Robinson and Ann Bryant at the Mississippi College (MC) Room. I owe many thanks to Bob and Lyda Gilmore: their kindness has been beyond measure. I am grateful to Cliff and Jayne Rushing for their 1950s images of Clinton.

I appreciate Norman Gough and Dr. Ed McMillan for their help with my work. I want to thank Dr. Walter Howell, former mayor; John H. Fox III, former city attorney; and Robert Wall, former photographer for the Clinton Chamber of Commerce. I owe many thanks to historian Shirley Faucette for her scholarship on Clinton. I am also grateful to Wyatt Waters, Ed McDonald, Debbie Tillman, Diane Newman-Carson, and Jan Nieminen at the Clinton Chamber of Commerce; Charlene McCord at the Arts Council of Clinton; Ryan Kelly; David and Mary Fehr; Marc Ridge; and all of the Clinton churches.

Abbreviations guide:
      Mississippi College, MC
      Mississippi Department of Archives and History, MDAH

INTRODUCTION

I had originally intended to give this volume the name *Clinton: Living History*. After a discussion with my editor, we decided it best to give this book a more chronological title, *Clinton: 1940–1980*. However, while my original title is physically gone, the phrase "living history" still resonates through the pages of this new Clinton book for several reasons.

One obvious reason why this history is living is because most of the Clintonians who have provided the pictures and history that fill these pages still live, thrive, and are, in many cases, the same individuals who brought about the momentous changes covered in this book. However, another reason why history lives is more applicable to the daily life of all Clintonians: this era of Clinton's history is lived day to day by all Clintonians who worship in the church buildings, attend schools in buildings, drive on the same roads, build houses in the neighborhoods, and start businesses in the same zones created in this historical era. Everyday in every way we live this history.

Clinton, Mississippi, is directly adjacent to Jackson, the capital of Mississippi. Most Mississippians (as well as some present-day Clintonians) think they know Clinton. Ask a Clintonian, and he or she will probably quote such statistics as the city's population of 23,347, a sizable urban area for rural Mississippi. Other new Clintonians might ebulliently add that their suburban mecca is the most prominent "bedtime community" within the Jackson metropolitan area, which numbers about 400,000 residents. The new Clintonian who habitually reads the *Wall Street Journal* might focus on the city's economic eminence: Clinton is home to companies such as Delphi Corporations-Packard Electric Systems and a branch office of MCI/SkyTel. Many new Clintonians will mention the city's Level 5 public school system and Mississippi College, Clinton's historic institution of higher learning.

However, beneath the surface of commercial sprawl and urban flight is a unique and independent history, and Clinton's past coexists with its present. World War II was the event that did more to change Clinton than perhaps even the Civil War. Several of Clinton's finest citizens, such as Dr. E. D. Reynolds, became leaders in the military. Others, such as Ed McDonald, came to Clinton to enroll in the U.S. Navy V12 officer training at Mississippi College and later settled in the area.

Clinton also housed about 3,000 German POWs at Camp Clinton. However, after the war, its effects continued to ripple for Clinton. In 1940, Clinton had a population of 916, and no property had been added to the town for almost 100 years. However, from 1940 to 1960, Clinton's population increased to 3,438, and the city's population doubled in both the 1970 and 1980 censuses. If the antebellum period was Clinton's boom, then the 1950s and 1960s was its bang. Postwar growth transformed Clinton from a small, independent community and college town into a modern suburban center. The first reason for this growth was that veterans, such as war hero Carey Ashcraft and his family, decided to make Clinton their new home. Secondly, as Jackson grew into a modern city with all the benefits and problems that accompanies growth, Clinton's future was also ineluctably changed. Clinton's independent sense of community began to be marked through its schools, businesses, and neighborhoods.

During World War II, Clinton had a military importance as a housing place for German prisoners of war captured in the North African desert. Most of the POWs came from Erwin Rommel's Afrika Korps. Camp Clinton was a detaining place for some of the most important German POWs, holding 35 of the 40 German generals captured by Allied forces. After World War II, Clinton enjoyed new growth and development, and Mississippi College grew with more students enrolling on the GI Bill. Many who came to Clinton to work at the POW camp or to attend Mississippi College after the war became Clintonians.

Images of America: Clinton: 1940–1980 captures a piece of each era of Clinton's past. Clinton's past is a chronicle that belongs to Clintonians—new and old alike.

One

A FINEST HOUR
WORLD WAR REACHES CLINTON

Dr. H. T. Ashford (left) and Pettigrew Warren pose for this triumphant photograph, their 20 mallards tied to Dr. Ashford's car. In 1940, life in Clinton had changed little since the Civil War. The town had put precious little new property inside its borders in 80 years, and most Clinton families had lived there for generations. Suddenly in 1942, the small southern town was thrust into the forefront of changing times. Many of Clinton's young men went to Europe and Asia to fight for American freedom. During World War II, Clinton also housed German POWs captured in North Africa and in the eastern Mediterranean, and Mississippi College was used as a U.S. Navy V12 school designed to train young men to be naval officers. However, this all would have seemed a fitful dream to Clintonians in 1940 whose lives had changed little. (Courtesy of Lyda Gilmore.)

Mississippi College faculty and students gather in force for this prewar photograph on the steps of the First Baptist Church in Clinton. For Clintonians (and Americans for that matter), Europe and Asia were far in the distance, the Pacific and Atlantic Oceans wide, and the world was an

enormous place. While, in the words of Mississippi playwright Tennessee Williams, "all the world was waiting for bombardments," life was quiet, calm, and unchanging in thousands of such American small towns. (Courtesy of Mississippi College.)

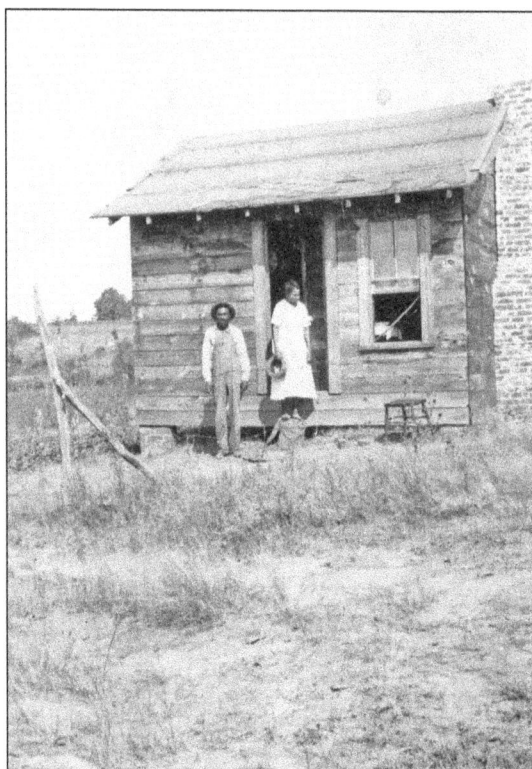

When it comes to the American South, changes often happen at a slow, gradual pace. An African American couple stands outside of an old wooden cabin that was once situated on the once-sprawling grounds of the Johnston House. For generations, poor whites and blacks lived on the same ancestral lands and large estates farmed by their grandfathers. The "Bulldozer Revolution" in the 1930s and 1940s across the South gave the more ambitious members of the farming and sharecropping class a way toward economic advancement, but Mississippi's economy remained largely dependent on agriculture. (Courtesy of Lyda Gilmore.)

Dr. H. T. Ashford was the town practitioner for years in Clinton. Dr. Ashford's old, black doctor's bag can often be seen at the Clinton Visitor Center on Pinehaven Road just off of the Natchez Trace. (Courtesy of Lyda Gilmore.)

In the photograph above, V12 cadets assemble on the Mississippi College campus grounds for inspection. As the United States militarily mobilized in the early 1940s for war, the armed forces decided they would need a larger, officer-training program to command the armies and navies that were swelling with newly enlisted men. Mississippi College was one of 1,600 institutions that applied for a U.S. Navy V12 program and one of the 131 institutions that were selected nationwide. In the below photograph, naval officers and non-commissioned officers stand on the steps of Jennings Hall on the day of inspection. (Both courtesy of MC.)

Above, naval V12 cadets participate in a rope climbing exercise in the gymnasium. Mississippi College had two physical-education instructors in the early 1940s, but both were serving in the military, and the college-sponsored athletics were almost nonexistent during the war years. However, the navy had its own physical training program for its cadets, and any civilian who wished to could participate with the naval trainees. Below, the cadets practice their swimming and diving skills. (Both courtesy of MC.)

In the above photograph, one of the V12 cadets drops back to throw a pass in a rare football game during the World War II years. This summer game was a time of fun in the midst of the shadow of world war. Pictured (right) in the college gymnasium, some of the cadets show off their dunking ability in a game of basketball. (Both courtesy of MC.)

Cadets from various classes and squads pose at attention on the steps of the Clinton Baptist Church (now the First Baptist Church of Clinton). On July 1, 1943, three hundred thirty-five men enrolled for the first term of the V12 training at Mississippi College (MC). The cadets were given full usage of Chrestman Dormitory, Alumni Hall, and the cafeteria. The V12 school was vital to the survival of the college during the war years. MC president Dr. Dot Nelson reported that 61 percent of the college's income was provided by the U.S. Navy. Because of the presence of the navel V12 School, the MC faculty was better prepared to work with a new generation of students who came to college courtesy of the GI Bill. (Both courtesy of MC.)

Here is a perimeter view of the Camp Clinton prisoner of war camp from Tower No. 7. Cameras were not allowed in the camp, but several guards and at least one prisoner, Otto W. Dopheide, snuck them into the camp for these photographs. At Camp Clinton, a few prisoners dug a tunnel about 100 feet long to try and escape under these double fences. Similar to their American POW counterparts in Germany, they hid the tunnel dirt in their pants legs and scattered it around the prison grounds, and found a way to install light bulbs to illuminate the tunnel. However, the prisoners were discovered by the guards when they were just 10 feet from the fence. (Courtesy of MDAH.)

17

In the above photograph, Private Benoit practices with his rifle and bayonet outside the Camp Clinton barracks. Below, Privates Bnusi (left) and Doyle guard one of the barracks. Clinton was one of four POW camps in Mississippi where prisoners were brought to the state to replenish a labor shortage caused by near-universal military enlistments. Most of the German POWs who came to Mississippi in 1943 were captured in North Africa while serving in Field Marshall Erwin Rommel's excellent Afrika Korps desert force. While most of the prisoners were happy with the good food and safe conditions free from the dangers of war, they remained elite soldiers to be guarded carefully. Early on, there was a need to protect the prisoners from each other as some of the political Nazis harassed and later murdered a German soldier. After this incident, the army intervened and sent the Nazis to a separate camp in Oklahoma, and tensions at Camp Clinton eased. (Both courtesy of MDAH.)

In the photograph above, Sgt. Henry Fonger mans Tower No. 7 with his submachine gun. Below, several German prisoners take a break with their escort for this photograph. The Geneva Convention did not allow the American army to force German officers to work, but it did allow them to work the enlisted German soldiers as long as their labor did not benefit the American war cause directly against their homeland. The prisoners were paid 90¢ a day for their labor and worked at picking cotton, clearing pulpwood, and planting trees, and some of the POWs helped to build the Mississippi River Basin Model for the U.S. Army Corps of Engineers. (Both courtesy of MDAH.)

Henry Fonger, wearing his briefs and a hard hat, and two other military policemen share in a bit of barracks jocularity during an easy day of work at Camp Clinton. Cameras and photographs were expressly forbidden inside the camp. However, unless a senior inspection officer was visiting or on duty, it can be deduced from the obvious easiness of the men (and their outfits) that the "no cameras or pictures" rule was, quite often, not rigorously kept. (Courtesy of MDAH.)

Above, Capt. Ernest Reynolds of Clinton (pictured far right) served in the Pacific as an army physician during World War II. Here he works at his headquarters in New Georgia. After the war, Dr. Reynolds returned home to his 49-year practice, during which he delivered 2,000 babies and sometimes accepted farm commodities for his physician's fee. Dr. Reynolds was also for racial equality, and though he was forced to bow to the social conventions and have two waiting rooms—one for whites and one for blacks—he cared for all his patients with the same professionalism and compassion. In the photograph below, Lt. Carey Ashcraft sees frontline action in Italy with the 88th Division. Ashcraft was captured by German forces on September 21, 1944, north of Florence. He and his fellow American POWs were liberated by the Russians on April 29, 1945, which happened to be the very day that German leader Adolf Hitler committed suicide. Today he and his wife, Delva, attend Dayspring Community Church faithfully each Sunday and enjoy visits with their grandchildren. (Above, courtesy of the Reynolds family; below, courtesy of Carey Ashcraft.)

Clinton's first baby boomers began to appear as soon as its men returned to their homes and their families. Pictured left, sisters Edith Johnston (on swing) and Lyda Johnston (far right) and young Chip "Chippy" Reynolds play on their playground set near West Leake Street. Below is a picture of West Leake Street in the late 1940s. (Both courtesy of Lyda Gilmore.)

Jannelle Landrum holds her cat Buster in front of the water tower near Olde Towne Clinton. (Courtesy of Lyda Gilmore.)

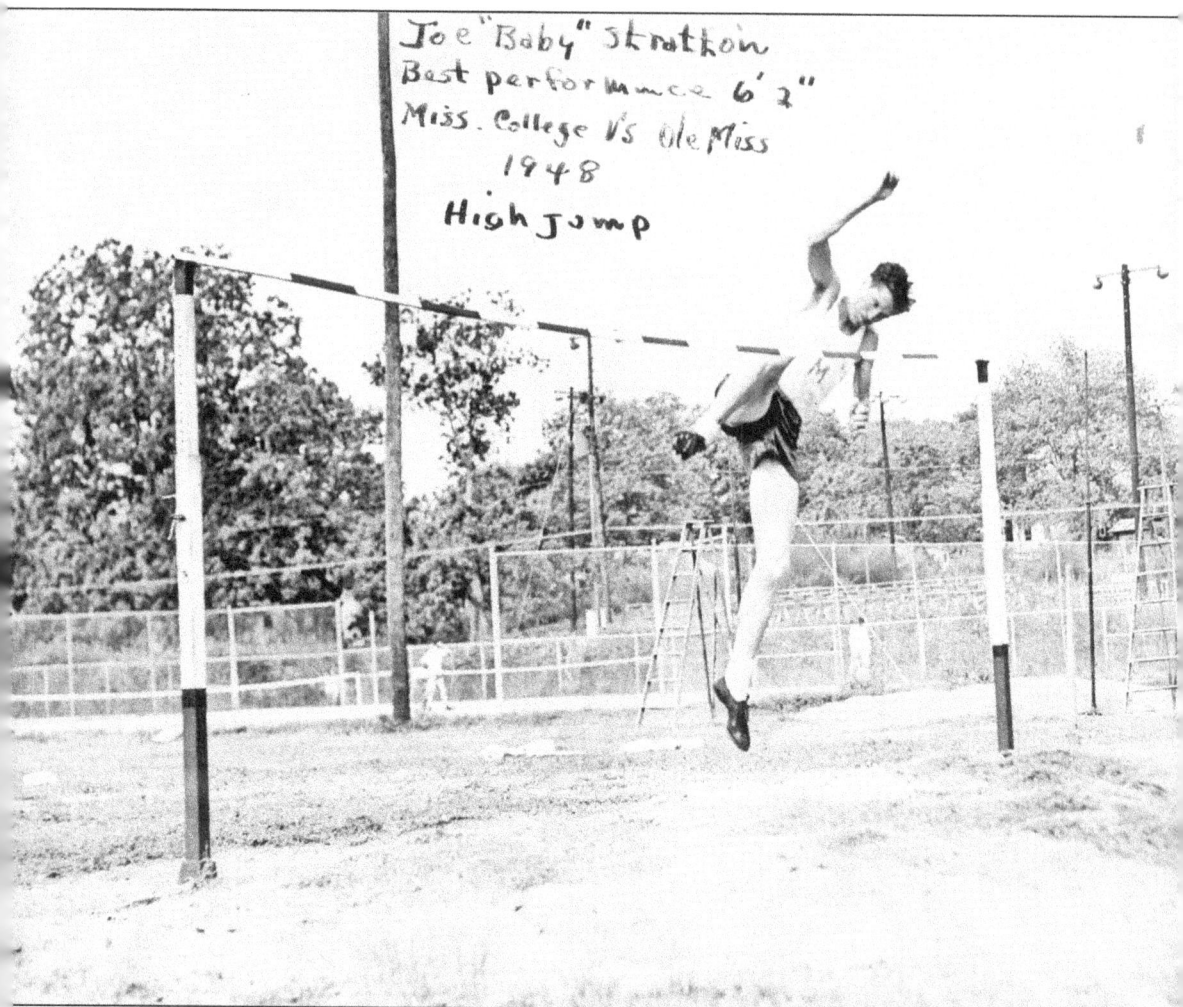

Joe "Baby" Stratton
Best performance 6' 2"
Miss. College Vs Ole Miss
1948
High Jump

Mississippi College track jumper Joe "Baby" Stratton displays his high jump on Robinson Field. Stratton's best performance was 6 feet 2 inches when the Choctaws played the Ole Miss Rebels in 1948. (Courtesy of MC.)

Two

GOLDEN YEARS
CLINTON IN THE 1950s
AND 1960s

Clinton elementary school students put on a play for President's Day in the early 1950s. Lyda Gilmore thinks that this annual event was special because it observed the first year Alaska and Hawaii were the 49th and 50th states. (Courtesy of Lyda Gilmore.)

While Clinton is often thought of as a Baptist town today, in the late 1950s, the Clinton Baptist Church (First Baptist today) was the only major Baptist congregation in the city. However, in 1958, members of the Clinton Baptist Church began a missionary church on an empty lot off of Highway 80 and Clinton Boulevard. The mission later became Morrison Heights Baptist Church. Pictured is Leura Myrtle Latimer, the widow of Mississippi College professor and Clinton mayor Murray Latimer. Latimer was the daughter of former MC president Rev. Warren Webb. The photograph was taken at the building site of Morrison Heights. (Courtesy of MC.)

In 1953, the Clinton third-grade class visited to the WLBT television station. (Courtesy of Lyda Gilmore.)

Pictured from left to right, Robert Johnston, Frank Stovall, and an unidentified man stand outside a store on a summer afternoon in downtown Clinton. (Courtesy of Lyda Gilmore.)

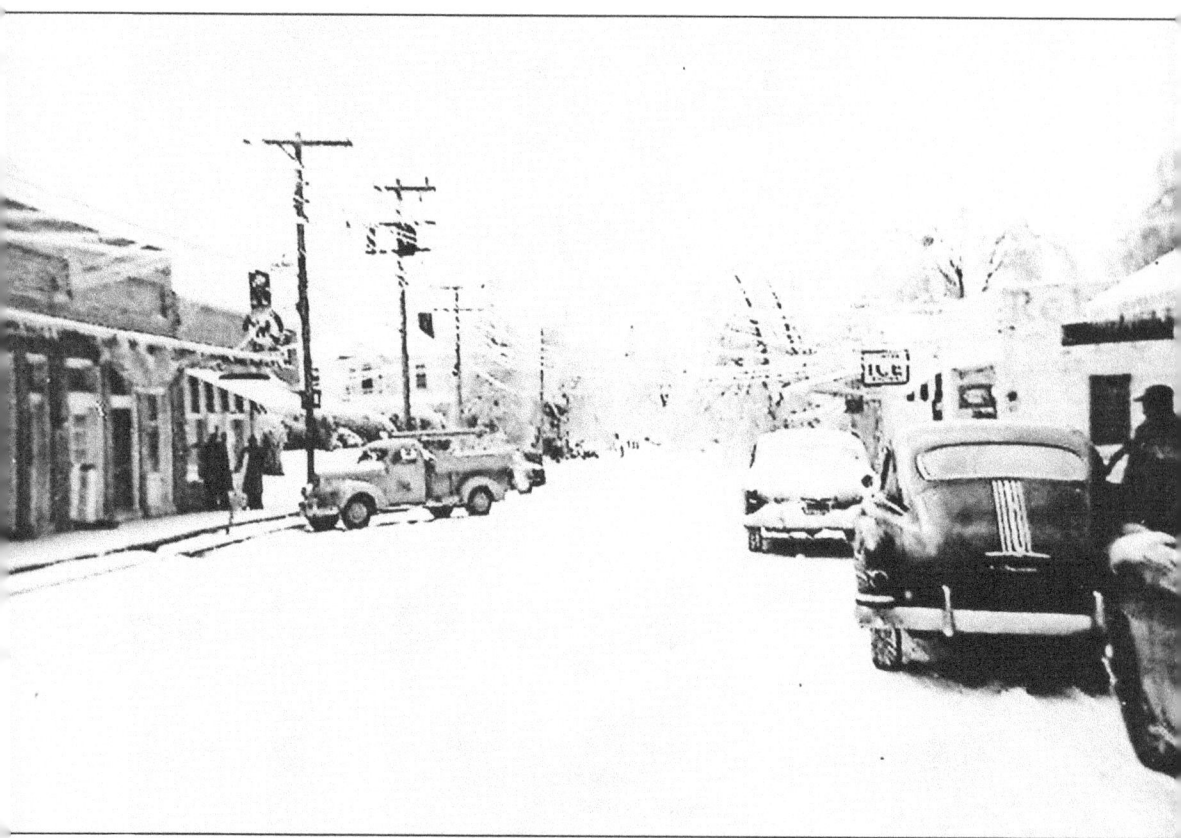

The 1951 snowstorm is marked in the minds of many Clintonians as one of the most remarkable in local history. Snow is so unusual in Mississippi that personal photograph collections in the state are often filled with images of snow. The lens of this photographer captures a splendid view of Jefferson Street heading south to Mississippi College where Nelson Hall stands in the center of the photograph just above the tree line. It is easy to physically reconstruct Clinton in 1951 from the snowstorm pictures. (Courtesy of Cliff and Jayne Rushing.)

Two young Clintonians enjoy a rare snowy day in front of the Potter House on Monroe Street. The Potter House was later moved to a lot across the street, and the new Clinton Police Department was constructed on the old Potter lot. (Courtesy of Cliff and Jayne Rushing.)

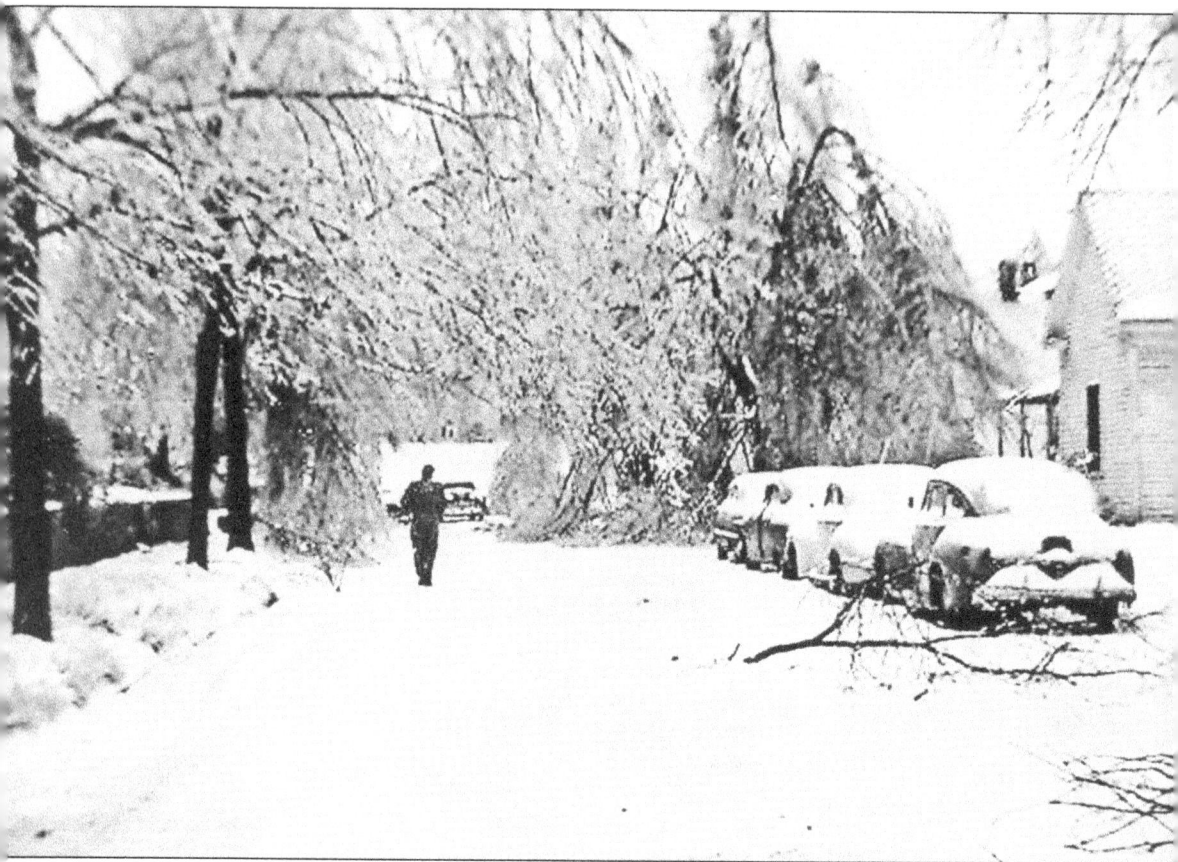

Snow is falling, branches are collapsing, and ears and fingers are freezing on this cold winter day in 1951. Fairmont Street near the old high school is covered in ice and snow. (Courtesy of Cliff and Jayne Rushing.)

Above, this was the home of S. M. Crain, the principal of Clinton High School in 1951. This house still exists on the property of the old Clinton Junior High School on Fairmont Street. In the 1980s, this was the home of Billy Ray Smith, then the junior high principal and a future Clinton mayor. In the image below, Mississippi College students gather above the steps leading to the college at the end of Jefferson Street. (Both courtesy of Cliff and Jayne Rushing.)

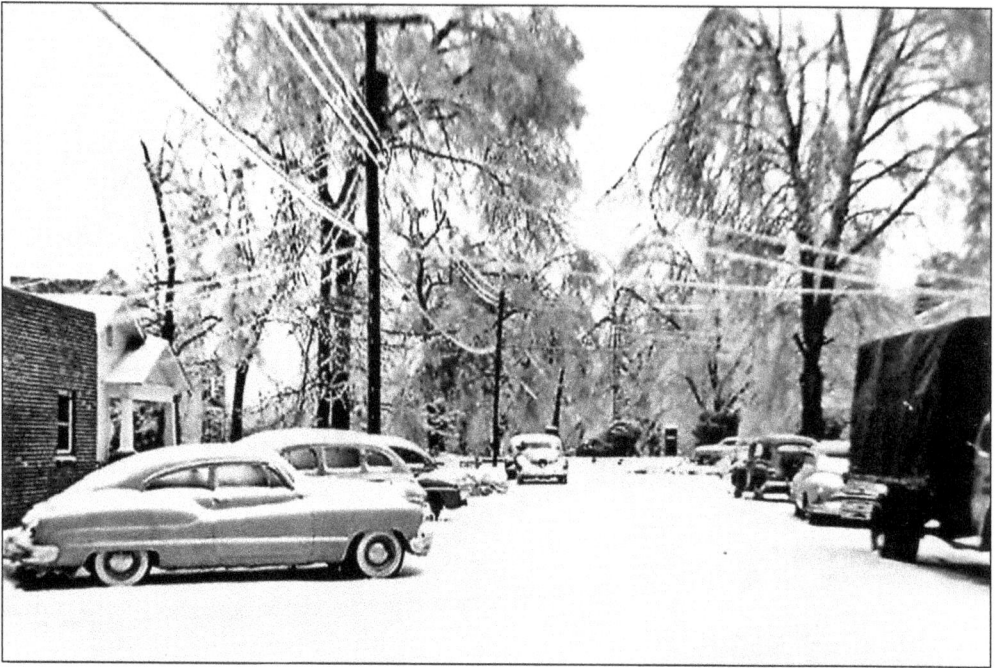

The photograph above was taken by someone standing in the middle of Monroe Street facing the old Hillman College campus, which is now Lyons Club Park. The photographer here is facing east. In the photograph below, the photographer turned to face south down Monroe Street. Obscured by the icy foliage, on the right incline is the old Clinton Methodist Church building where the Choctaw Apartments are today. (Both courtesy of Cliff and Jayne Rushing.)

The picture above was taken from the front of the Potter House at the intersection of Monroe and East Leake Streets. For the photograph below, the photographer turned completely around to face north. The covered truck to the left in the distance is near the spot where the three previous photographs were taken. To the right above the car is the Potter House. (Both courtesy of Cliff and Jayne Rushing.)

The Clinton High School BETA club sits in the Mississippi College bleachers for this photograph, perhaps before a Clinton Arrows football game. In the early 1950s, all Clinton High School football games were played at the old Choctaw football stadium that has since been torn down to make room for the modern Baptist Healthplex. (Courtesy of Cliff and Jayne Rushing.)

Above, Clinton Arrows football captains Gerald Pevey (left) and Charles Baggett pose for this photograph on their practice field. Pevey was starting tackle for the Arrows, and Bagget was a starting back. Both are members of the Clinton High School class of 1954. Collegiate football players were beginning to wear tear-away jerseys, an innovation that allowed running backs to rush for thousand yard seasons because their expanding jerseys could rip right through the hands of defensive linemen. However, in 1954, the Clinton Arrows still wore the old jerseys, which meant that an Arrows running back or receiver had to work for every yard he earned. Below, Charles Harrison (left) and James Rankin pose in a silly shot before a Clinton Arrows football game. Harrison's hat is supposed to be a chicken, which he wore as part of a school fund-raiser. Since there was little money in the school's budget for extracurricular activities, the students had several fund-raisers each year. (Both courtesy of Cliff and Jayne Rushing.)

The 1953 Clinton Arrows football team was indeed small, which means many on the team played both offense and defense, and the key to victory lay equally in durability as well as athletic skill. The above photograph was taken beside John H. Treelore's house, which is still situated on the campus of the old Clinton Junior High School. The program below chronicles the Homecoming game the Arrows played against the Canton Panthers at Mississippi College's Robinson Field on October 19, 1953. (Both courtesy of Cliff and Jayne Rushing.)

HOMECOMING ACTIVITIES

7:45—Coronation Ceremony

Homecoming Queen	Miss Billie Jean Barnett
Maid of Honor	Miss Shirley McCoy
Sr. Maid	Miss Nancy Owings
Jr. Maid	Miss Ann Blakeny
Soph. Maid	Miss Betty Bostic
Fresh. Maid	Miss Kathryn Scott

Captain	Lowell Livingston

Escorts	Mr. Roger Alford
	Mr. Paul Murrill
	Mr. James Rees
	Mr. Robert Causey
	Mr. Joe Ben Alley
	Mr. Lane Arbuthnot

8:00—Clinton vs Canton

At the Half—A performance by the Clinton and Canton Bands.

After the Game—A reception in the High School cafeteria for teachers, students, the team, former students, parents and friends of the School.

Programs Compliments of
THE CLINTON NEWS
The only Newspaper in the World devoted entirely to the welfare of Clinton, Miss

CLINTON
HIGH
SCHOOL

HOMECOMING

Clinton Arrows
vs
Canton Panthers

7:45 P.M. FRIDAY, OCT. 19

ROBINSON FIELD
CLINTON, MISSISSIPPI

FOREST HILL vs CLINTON
Forest Hill Football Field
September 18--8 P. M.

FOREST HILL			CLINTON		
NO.	NAME	POSITION	NO.	NAME	POSITION
20	Freddie Hutton	Back	00	Joel Hollingsworth	End
21	Gaines Osburne	Back	00	Ray Hudson	End
22	Edgar Sanford	Back	00	Roy Hall	Back
23	Jo Jeff Fulmer	Back	11	A. B. Bryant	End
24	James Lewis	Back	14	Cliff Rushing	Back
25	Cooter Harmon	Back	17	Jack McDonald	Back
26	J. D. Wright	Guard	18	Pete Magoun	Guard
27	Wayne Wallace	End	19	Gerald Miles	Back
28	Jerry Hutchinson	End	20	Stan Rushing	Center
29	Jack Tyson	End	21	Jimmy Anderson	Back
30	Billy Rhymes	Guard	24	Jimmy Dillard	Tackle
31	James Bryant	Back	25	Gerald Pevey	Tackle
32	Thomas Derrick	Tackle	26	Ralph Magoun	Tackle
33	Quinton Floyd	Tackle	27	Tom Willette	Tackle
34	Bob Whitfield	Tackle	29	Jack Quick	Back
35	Bill Hendee	End	30	Marlain Cox	Guard
36	Max Davis	Guard	32	Peter Russell	Guard
37	Billy Parker	Center	32	Pat Walker	Guard
38	Charles Watson	Guard	36	Albert Green	Tackle
39	Monte Cook	Center	37	Byrd Allen	Guard
40	Don Sharp	Tackle	37	Buddy Douglas	Tackle
41	Whimpy Martin	Tackle	38	Bobby Miles	Guard
BLUE UNIFORMS			39	Don Majors	End
26	Bobby Bryant	Back	40	Charles McCollum	Center
28	Eugene Adcock	Back	41	Charles Baggett	Back
32	Arlen Barrett	Back	42	Jerry Ivy	Back
39	Eudene Adcock	End	43	Charles Gilmore	Back
43	Don Taylor	Tackle	44	Dan Cleveland	Tackle
			45	Smut Saik	End
			46	Charles Pevey	End

COACH: RAY BELL
ASST. COACH: CHAS. CALLOWAY

MGRS: CARL LEWIS
      JOHN L. SULLIVAN

COACHES: GENE KITCHENS,
    G. CRONIA, J. McDANIEL
MANAGERS: JIMMIE STREET
    STEVE BRASFIELD

FOREST HILL SCHEDULE

September 25	Morton at Forest Hill	8:00 P. M.
October 2	Forest Hill at Prentiss	
October 9	Mendenhall at Forest Hill	7:30 P. M.
October 16	Forest Hill at Pearl	
October 23	Forest Hill at Magee	
October 30	Byram at Forest Hill	7:30 P. M.
November 6	Forest Hill at Brandon	
November 13	Crystal Springs at F. Hill	7:30 P. M.

The roster for the Forest Hill Rebels and Clinton Arrows game marks one of the greatest high-school rivalries in the Jackson Metro area. On the Forest Hill roster, it is noticeable that some of the Rebels were to wear "blue uniforms" separately from the rest of their team. (Courtesy of Cliff and Jayne Rushing.)

In the left photograph, Delores Cox was the head drum majorette during the 1953 Arrows football season. Below, Evelyn Porch was a Clinton High School cheerleader and the senior class secretary for the 1953–1954 school year. (Both courtesy of Cliff and Jayne Rushing.)

Clinton High School (CHS) girls sit on the hill overlooking Robinson Field at Mississippi College to watch a CHS track meet. Some of those pictured are Martha Landrum, Maxine Kelly, Evelyn Porch, Melvia Landrum, Joyce Nall, Jo Nall, Charlene Kelly, and Mamie Reese. In the group there are two pairs of sisters, and the girls here represent the CHS classes of 1951, 1952, 1953, and 1954. (Courtesy of Cliff and Jayne Rushing.)

Evelyn Porch (left) displays her cheerleading skirt to sisters Maxine Kelly (center) and Charlene Kelly. (Courtesy of Cliff and Jayne Rushing.)

Several members of the Clinton High School faculty gather at Robinson Field to observe and assist in an unusual fund-raiser: a girls' football game. From left to right, the teachers are unidentified, Elenor Polk, J. Hutchinson, Mattie Lee Burris, Nell Potter, and J. King. Mattie Burris (pictured below) served as the line judge for the girls' football game. (Both courtesy of Cliff and Jayne Rushing.)

Pictured above, Cliff Rushing and Jayne Embry enjoy a trip to Roosevelt State Park with other Clinton football players in the fall of 1952. Today Cliff and Jayne are married and still live in Clinton. In the left image, Gerald Pevey (left) and Floyd Jones both enjoy the atmosphere of Roosevelt State Park and the company of their Arrows friends. (Both courtesy of Cliff and Jayne Rushing.)

Bryant   Gladys Hall   James Rankin,V.Pres   Evelyn Porch,Secty   Cliff Rushing,Pres   Karlene Stafford,Treas   Pete Magoun   Sue Parkman   Gerald Pevey

Hollingsworth   Sandra Sumrall   Emile Saik   Joyce Nall   Gordon DeMent   Betty Bostic   Charles Baggett   Shirley Hales

Douglas   Rachel Hudson   Marianne Bowering   Dolores Cox

Clinton High School

Class of 1954

Kelly   Charlie Triplett   Fredna Vaughn   Tom Willetts   Carolyn Griffis   David Abernathy   Resa Mae Dowdy   Bill Speed   Martha Landrum

Jorgensen   Ann Hall   Edna Garraway   Virginia Williams   Jeff Bell   Betty Jo Thompson   Joan Roberts   Gail Miller   Betty Jo Simon

The size of the 1954 graduating class is representative of the size of the student body in the early 1950s: small and closely knit. It was extremely easy for everyone to know each member of their graduating class, and most class members continued to keep in contact long after leaving Clinton High School with their diplomas. By the 1970s and 1980s, the atmosphere had changed considerably in the Clinton public schools. In 1996, the Clinton High School graduating class went from 50 to 303 students, an increase of nearly 500 percent. (Courtesy of Cliff and Jayne Rushing.)

The old Clinton High School was located between College and Fairmont Streets east of Mississippi College. After 1964, high school students went to the new school building on Lakeview Drive where it stayed until 1996. The old high school building continued to be used for the junior high until 1996, when it was moved to Lakeview Drive and the high school was moved to Arrow Drive off of Pinehaven Road. Today this building is used for the alternative school. (Courtesy of Cliff and Jayne Rushing.)

Pictured right, Mickey DeWitt (now
Landrum) stands outside city hall with
Mattie Lee Burris (right), a mathematics
teacher and yearbook editor. Shown
below, Sue Parkman sits on a swing
set on the northeast side of the then
Clinton High School campus. (Both
courtesy of Cliff and Jayne Rushing.)

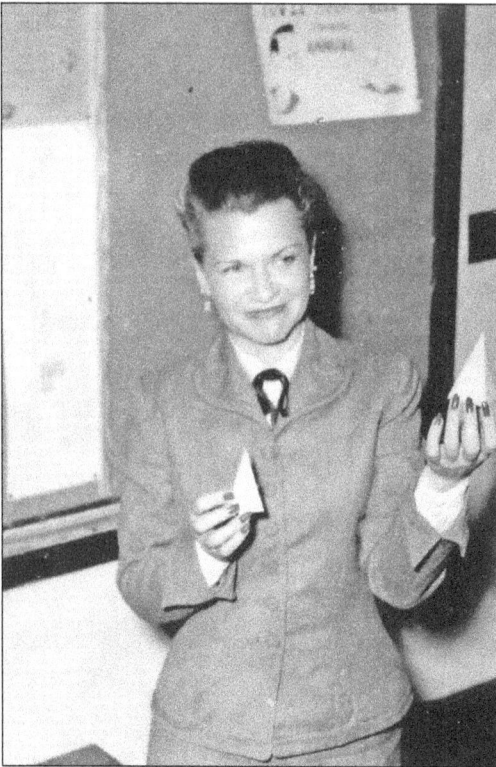

Mattie Lee Burris, a Clinton High School math and geometry teacher, is pictured as most of her students remember her: holding her paper-made geometric shapes. Burris was the head of the Clinton BETA club and also the editor of the *Arrowhead* annual. Below is an elegant picture of Burris in a lower-neckline gown. (Both courtesy of Cliff and Jayne Rushing.)

Mattie Lee Burris and her 1955 BETA club look up into the bleachers of the Clinton High School gymnasium while the photographer captures, in addition to the club, the amazing reflection of the gym floor. (Courtesy of Cliff and Jayne Rushing.)

Clinton High School students gather in the cafeteria for a fund-raiser in 1955, which, though long forgotten, obviously had a naval theme. (Courtesy of Cliff and Jayne Rushing.)

Mrs. J. Hutchinson, a Clinton High School English teacher, sits on the steps with the male members of the class of 1954 seniors. (Courtesy of Cliff and Jayne Rushing.)

Clinton High School juniors
A. B. Bryant and Evelyn Porch pose
outside the redbrick building during
another Arrows fund-raiser. (Courtesy
of Cliff and Jayne Rushing.)

Clinton High School BETA club
member Bud Walker poses with
Mary Ann Mobley (pictured right)
of Brandon, who became Miss
Mississippi in 1958 and was crowned
Miss America in 1959. Mobley later
made movie appearances with such
stars as Elvis Presley and made
appearances in television shows such
as *General Hospital* and *Love Boat*. The
other girl is unidentified. (Courtesy
of Cliff and Jayne Rushing.)

Mrs. H. Spell, Donald Bells, Mrs. Elley, and other guests often gathered together in the early 1950s on the lawn of Dr. Dot Nelson and his wife for special events and faculty tea parties. (Courtesy of MC.)

Mrs. Nelson (seated) welcomes members of the American Association of University Women (AAUW) to her home for tea. Below, members of the AAUW gather for punch and pastries in 1955. The AAUW has been responsible for much service to the Clinton community, including a book entitled *Down Brick Streets* in 1976, which was a history of Clinton's historical homes and places. (Both courtesy of MC.)

In 1957, Dr. R. A. McLemore was a prominent Mississippi historian who had taken up the daunting task of writing a two-volume *History of Mississippi*, as well as a history of Southern Baptists. McLemore was also elected by the board of trustees to be the 15th president of Mississippi College in 1957. The picture here is unusual since Dr. Nelson's name, McLemore's predecessor, is still on the president's desk. (Courtesy of MC.)

Young Mississippi College scholars were honored in the library. The students pictured are, from left to right, Jeff Speed, Betsey Emerson, Nancy Farr, Caroline Walker, Vaughn Earl Hartzell, and Virginia O'Neal. The presenter is unidentified. (Courtesy of MC.)

Mississippi College team captain Fred Morris, in the above photograph holding the football, breaks free into the backfield of the opposing team to get the Choctaws a first down. Though this photograph was made in the 1950s, the Choctaw football players had yet to switch to the tear-away jerseys, which means Morris earned his break into the backfield. The 1950s were the golden age of college football and college athletics, and whenever teams traveled to other colleges for away games, many fans traveled with them. As the picture to the right indicates, the football season and the arrival of visiting teams and fans was a definite boon to the home community, and in the 1950s, the Choctaws were starting to travel well. (Both courtesy of MC.)

Above, Mississippi College students in 1958 were attending chapel services in Swore Auditorium in Nelson Hall. Enrollment had long increased, making campus-wide compulsory attendance inside the smaller, more historic Provine Chapel impossible. The audience represents a wide range of MC personalities. To the right, two seats behind Dr. Nelson and on the left end, is Dr. Howard Spell. A Bible professor and longtime academic dean of the college, Dr. Spell is revered today by students and faculty who knew him. However, three seats behind Dr. Spell is MC political science professor Dr. William Caskey who, according to students and colleagues, organized the local Citizens' Council in the 1950s and early 1960s. Below, the MC Tribal Players in 1964 enacted some of Shakespeare's plays, including *Hamlet*, the playwright's sprawling masterpiece. Dr. George Pittman was the Shakespearian professor of the English department, and he was heavily invested in some of these productions. (Both courtesy of MC.)

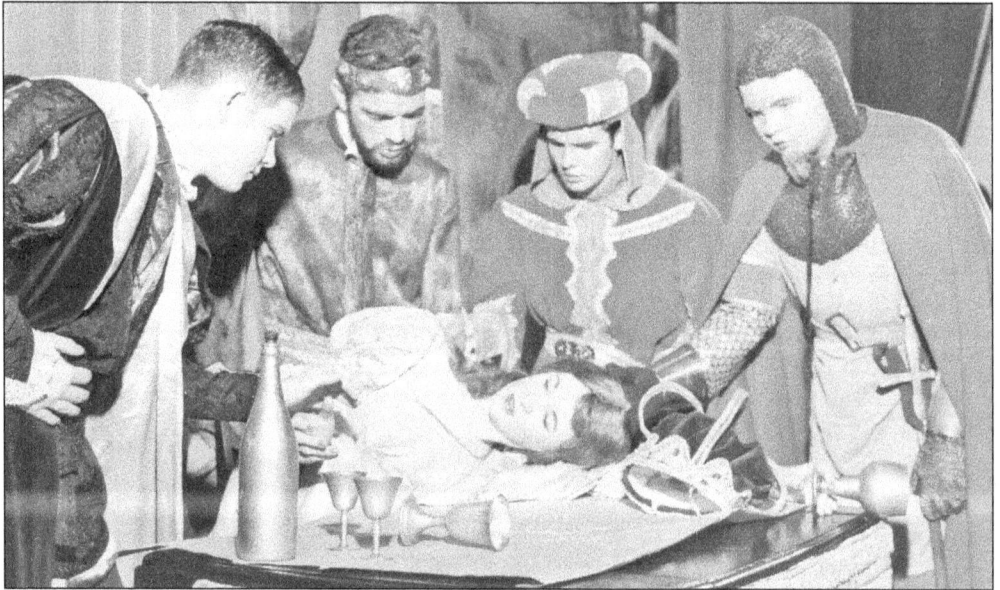

In the picture above, photographer Robert Wall captures the home of Dr. Howard Spell on College Street in rare winter splendor. Built around the 1920s, Dr. Spell and his wife moved into this house sometime in the 1940s. The snowy oaks in the front yard remind Dr. Spell's numerous friends of the educator's interest in woodcarving. Dr. Walter Howell, a MC history professor and longtime friend of Dr. Spell, became mayor of Clinton in 1981; Dr. Spell carved a gavel for him made from an old church pew. Dr. Spell especially delighted in using the wood from abandoned churches and church pews for his carving. As academic dean, Dr. Spell (pictured right) created a "Grade Distribution Chart" with data gathered from all the academic departments that Dr. Spell would present to the faculty to curb the nationwide trend of college grade inflation. (Above, courtesy of Robert Wall; below, courtesy of MC.)

The Mississippi College class of 1935 is reunited in 1965 for their 30-year reunion. While such a long period of time takes it toll on classmates, faculty members, and college staff, several of the old professors and dorm mothers from 1965 are seated in the first row with the class of 1935.

The Mississippi College they were returning to in 1965 was far different than the one they left in 1935, but as is often the case with smaller graduating classes, the bonds between classmates are personal. (Courtesy of MC.)

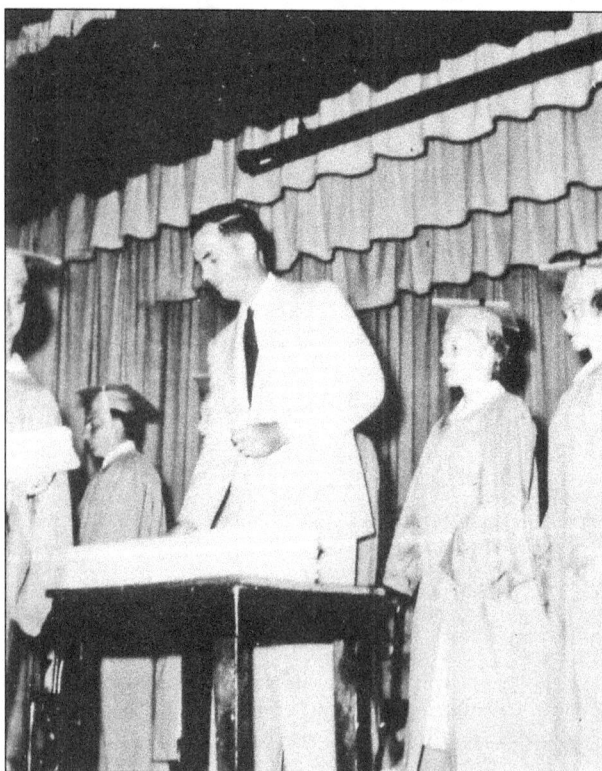

The class of 1963 was the first one to graduate from the new Clinton High School campus on Lakeview Drive. As enrollment within the Clinton public schools began to double and triple throughout the years, the school board added on to this building until 1996 when a new campus for high school students was opened on Arrow Drive near the Natchez Trace. In the left picture, John H. Treelore, Clinton High School agricultural teacher, hands out diplomas to the 1954 graduates. Treelore later left the Clinton public schools to be the principal of a private school in Jackson. (Both courtesy of Cliff and Jayne Rushing.)

The Clinton High School BETA club in the early 1960s poses for this school photograph at the old high school auditorium on Fairmont Street. (Courtesy of Lyda Gilmore.)

This Vacation Bible School (pictured above) was hosted each summer by Mount Salus Presbyterian Church, and children from outside the town of Clinton and the state of Mississippi were invited to attend the lessons. This 1968 bible school was directed by Anne Stather and Fannelle Shepperson of Camden, Arkansas. In the left photograph, Mount Salus children celebrate Christmas in their new Fellowship Hall in 1955. (Both courtesy of Mount Salus Presbyterian Church.)

In 1955, the new Mount Salus congregation celebrated their first Christmas in their new Fellowship Hall on College Street. Pictured from left to right are, in the back row standing, a Mrs. Mahaffery, Mary Melton, Billy Lumpkin, Emily Gage, Richard Foster, and Alice Fancher; on the back row seated, unidentified, Mrs. Robert Emanuel, Craig Emmanuel, Barbara Brett, Bruce Reynolds, Mrs. E. D. Reynolds, Mrs. G. R. Phillips, and G. Raymond Phillips; on the second row seated, R. L. Foster, Jennie Brett (hidden), Dianne Emmanuel, Sandra Emmanuel, Rick Ledbetter, Susan Emmanuel, Stokes Neal, and Debbie Reynolds; on the second row standing, LaBelle Sherer, Steve Sherer, Bill Brett, John Odeneal, and a Mr. Brett; on the third row seated, Mrs. George Neal, Don Neal, Barbara Ellen Neal, Bobby Odeneal, Judy Odeneal, Bunny Mahaffey, and Perry Egger. In the foreground is Chip Reynolds. (Courtesy of Mount Salus Presbyterian Church.)

In September 1958, the Dorcus Class of Morrison Heights Baptist Tent Ministry (pictured above) stopped for a quick snapshot after their Sunday lesson. Morrison Heights' tent ministry was on the eastern outskirts of Clinton. The massive Baptist church today at 201 Morrison Drive began as a missionary branch of the Clinton First Baptist Church on College Street, and Morrison Heights Baptist Church became independent in 1958 with 126 charter members. The men of the new Morrison Heights church took a "work day" on October 17, 1959, to pave the sidewalks and prepare for the opening of their new church (pictured below). (Both courtesy of Ed McDonald.)

In 1957, the young adults at Clinton Methodist Church drink Coca-Colas and engage in a lively Bible study. In the photograph below is Anne Powers Wood's Sunday School class in 1957. While Wood's husband, longtime Clinton mayor and MC chemistry professor A. E. Wood, was a staunch Baptist, she remained a Methodist and hosted this Sunday School class for senior citizens and retirees of the Clinton Methodist Church. (Both courtesy of the Clinton Methodist Church.)

Pictured from left to right, three men representing the Jitney Jungle corporation, architect Army Brown, an unidentified man, Dr. A. E. Wood, the brothers Dan and John Gore, and local realtor Ed McDonald break ground for the new Clinton Plaza in 1963. The plaza was the first of several

new suburban strip malls to sprawl forth from the undeveloped lands around Clinton. The shovels Brown and Wood are leaning on are engraved with the date and the shopping center's name. (Courtesy of Ed McDonald.)

Mississippi College president Dr. McLemore, Clinton mayor Dr. A. E. Wood, Taylor, Clinton alderman Howard Jones, architect Army Brown, J. R. Rankin, and Ed McDonald stand together on a platform on the opening day for the Clinton Plaza. In the photograph below, Army Brown, Dr. Wood, Dr. McLemore, and Ed McDonald participate in the Clinton Plaza ribbon-cutting ceremony. (Both courtesy of Ed McDonald.)

The old location of the College Cleaners was on College Street, and B. E. Martin operated the business. College Cleaners is today located near the intersection of New Prospect Street and Highway 80. (Courtesy of Robert Wall.)

The Clinton Police Department was once located in this small building just outside the city hall. When Clinton's population tripled in size during the 1960s and 1970s, its growing police force outgrew this quaint structure. (Courtesy of Robert Wall.)

Around the table (pictured above) is the board of the Capital Electric Power Association (CEPA), which provided power to the tri-county area, as well as Claiborne, Warren, and Sharkey Counties. CEPA was one of numerous rural electric associations started in the 1930s, subsidized by the federal government, and owned by local shareholders. CEPA and dozens of rural electric confederations were bought by Mississippi Power and Light. However, as the number of customers in the Jackson area grew in the 1960s, CEPA became a vital company. Members of the board are pictured from left to right: (first row) Howite Walcotte, Tommy Jones, and Hinds County schools superintendent W. W. Cain; (second row) a Vicksburg preacher, Billy Harrell, unidentified, Clinton realtor Ed McDonald, and Clinton resident Burt Cloud, who was elected president. Two Clintonians serving on the CEPA board signifies the city's newfound importance within the Jackson metropolitan area. However, Clinton's new economic avenues continued to coexist with its old. The Johnson Milling Company (pictured below) still operates near the spot where all of Clinton's old train depots existed. (Above, courtesy of Ed McDonald; below, courtesy of Robert Wall.)

Three

LIVING HISTORY
CLINTON BEYOND THE 1960s

Clinton spectators sit on a mound of grass (probably near what was the old high school and then junior high) on College Street and watch the homecoming parade in 1976. Since most Clintonians chose their city for a quiet life separate from the larger state capital of Jackson, many of them could have remained oblivious to the growth of their community until they visited one of the new shopping centers or attended one of Clinton's two annual parades or one of its two annual arts and crafts shows. (Courtesy of Robert Wall.)

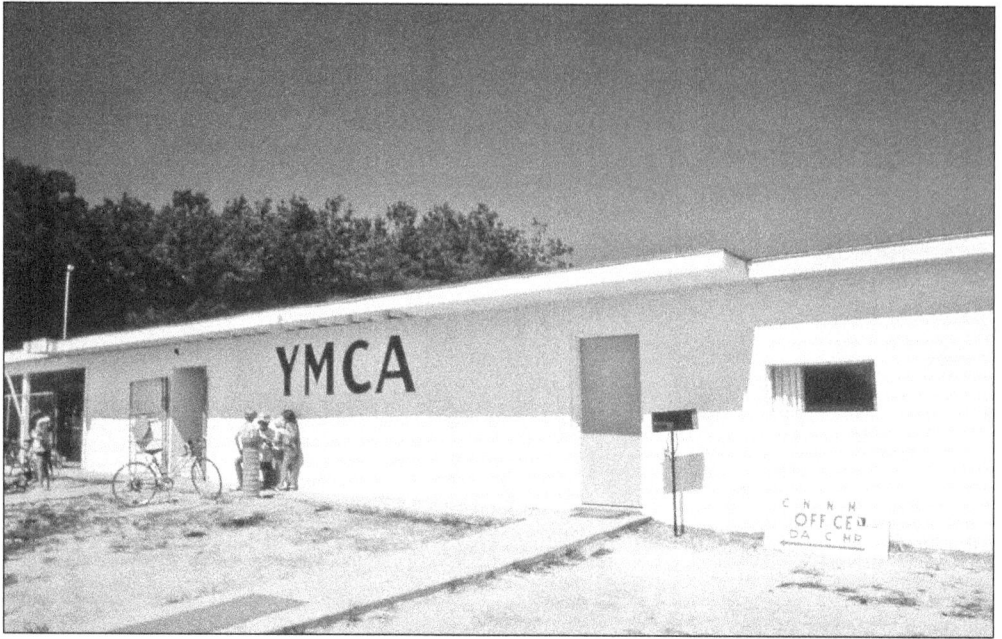

In the photograph above, the modern YMCA was built on Lindale Street where it remains today. While the Young Men's Christian Association has long been a part of Clinton, it was when the YMCA relocated to Lindale Street, where several large swimming pools (below) were built, that its membership grew. Both then and now, the YMCA pool offers activities and swimming lessons for Clinton's youth during the hot, humid summer months of June, July, and especially August. (Both courtesy of Robert Wall.)

In the 1970s, the Kentucky Fried Chicken (KFC) in Clinton was located on Clinton Boulevard. Since then, KFC has had two other locations, presently now on Highway 80 East. The original building in a reduced form still exists as an antiques store. An indelible image of Americana, the restaurant marks some of the first tides of Clinton's increasing growth and commercialization. (Courtesy of Robert Wall.)

A child goes sledding near Dunton Road, which is indeed a rare sight in normally hot, humid Mississippi. (Courtesy of Robert Wall.)

This view of the opposite side of the lake displays the Lakeview Heights neighborhood captures the quintessence of suburban, middle-class nostalgia. The developer was Siby McRee, who lived in Lakeview Heights near the lake, and his house was marked with many azaleas. (Courtesy of Robert Wall.)

As Clinton grew in population, wealth, and commercialization, its new citizens were often concerned with the present and its comforts, and with the future and the planning and zoning that it required. However, many Clintonians began to look toward the past. West of Clinton, the New Salem Cemetery still exists, but few can gain access to it; only by traversing jungles of tree saplings, broken trails, and deer paths can a lucky antiquarian find it. (Courtesy of Cliff and Jayne Rushing.)

Jayne Rushing cleans off one of the forgotten graves at the New Salem Cemetery. Jayne and her husband, Cliff, Clinton High School sweethearts from the 1950s, found the cemetery by accident while bird hunting with their dogs. While some of Clinton's history such as the Cedars, the Provine Chapel, and Tanglewood can be found by the cursory eye, much of Clinton's history is under the surface. Such discoveries are sometimes found with luck, but often it takes a dedicated antiquarian to bring such finds to light. (Courtesy of Cliff and Jayne Rushing.)

Despite Clinton's modern transformation from a small town to a modern suburban center, most of its honored traditions continued unabated. Pictured from left to right are Clinton Freemasons: (standing, first row) unidentified; Ed McDonald, international head of the Eastern Star; Clyde Canton; and Michell Crawford; (second row) Roy Duncan, Fred Drakewater, Joe Skee, and P. L. Hughes. (Courtesy of Ed McDonald.)

Larry Myricks attended Mississippi College in the late 1970s. Myricks became a record-breaking long jumper for the Choctaws, and he went on to be one of the greatest long jumpers in history. Myricks was an extremely durable athlete, and he made the U.S. Olympic team four times. For 13 consecutive years he recorded a jump of at least 27 feet. Myricks's sedulous training has carried him to three national championships, two World Cup titles, two World Championship bronze medals, and, in the 1988 Summer Olympics in Seoul, South Korea, Myricks earned a bronze medal. (Courtesy of MC.)

In 1984, Mayor Walter Howell worked to organize a Dewitt Clinton Celebration for April of that year, named for Gov. Dewitt Clinton of New York who dug the Erie Canal and for whom the town of Clinton was named. The Dewitt festival later became the Brick Street Festival, but one of the special Dewitt events was a Barry Hannah Day. In the picture above, Hannah stands below the banner artist Wyatt Waters painted for the event. Below, Barry Hannah speaks at the A. E. Wood Memorial Library in Clinton. Aside from *Geronimo Rex*, his first novel based on Clinton, Hannah has a body of work including novellas such as *Ray* and story collections such as *Airships*, which helped Hannah earn the Award for Literature from the American Institute of Arts and Letters. Hannah has also been nominated for the Pulitzer Prize. Hannah today holds the position of writer-in-residence at Ole Miss. (Both courtesy of Charlene McCord.)

This aerial photograph of the central part of Mississippi College's campus captures the grounds where the fall Arts and Crafts Festival is held each September. The festival was then sponsored by the Junior Civic League but is now sponsored by the Arts Council of Clinton. The fall Arts and Crafts Festival is one of two festivals for the arts hosted in Clinton annually. (Courtesy of MC.)

This photograph from a lower altitude, possibly from the student center, shows the festival in full swing. For years, the Clinton Arts and Crafts Festival took place on the campus grounds of Mississippi College. Artists and artisans alike set up booths to sell their wares, and there was always food and music. Today the Arts and Crafts Festival takes place on Jefferson Street on the brick streets of Olde Towne Clinton. (Courtesy of Robert Wall.)

A multitude of artisans in booths display their wares in front of Nelson Hall in the 1970s. Visited not only by students and Clintonians, the festival is also attended by people who come from all over Mississippi and the Southeast to mingle with artisans, craftsmen, and aficionados of handmade crafts. Visitors at the festival can find anything from ceramics, woodcarvings, dolls, baskets, and children's toys. Food is also for sale in the form of burgers, hotdogs, and boiled peanuts. (Both courtesy of Robert Wall.)

At a booth (above) in the 1970s, two Civil War antiquarians display recovered Confederate and Federal artifacts found around Clinton and in Hinds and Warren Counties. Stationed at an angle from Nelson Hall (pictured below), women at another booth display cloth dolls and flowers. (Both courtesy of Robert Wall.)

Most of the booths at the fall Arts and Crafts Festival are mere tables and canopied tents. However, some of the designs are unique. At this booth in the 1970s, a visitor could purchase a special recipe of black-eyed peas in addition to other country home items. (Courtesy of Robert Wall.)

Above, at a booth situated across College Street obliquely angled from the First Baptist Church of Clinton, several women and children look at hand-carved chess and checker figures. The artisan has undoubtedly stepped away from the booth, and a young girl is there to take money or answer questions. Just as it was in the 1970s, the festival is an informal affair. Below, directly in front of the college library, a visitor looks at a painting of a steamboat, one of hundreds of individual art pieces for sale that day. (Both courtesy of Robert Wall.)

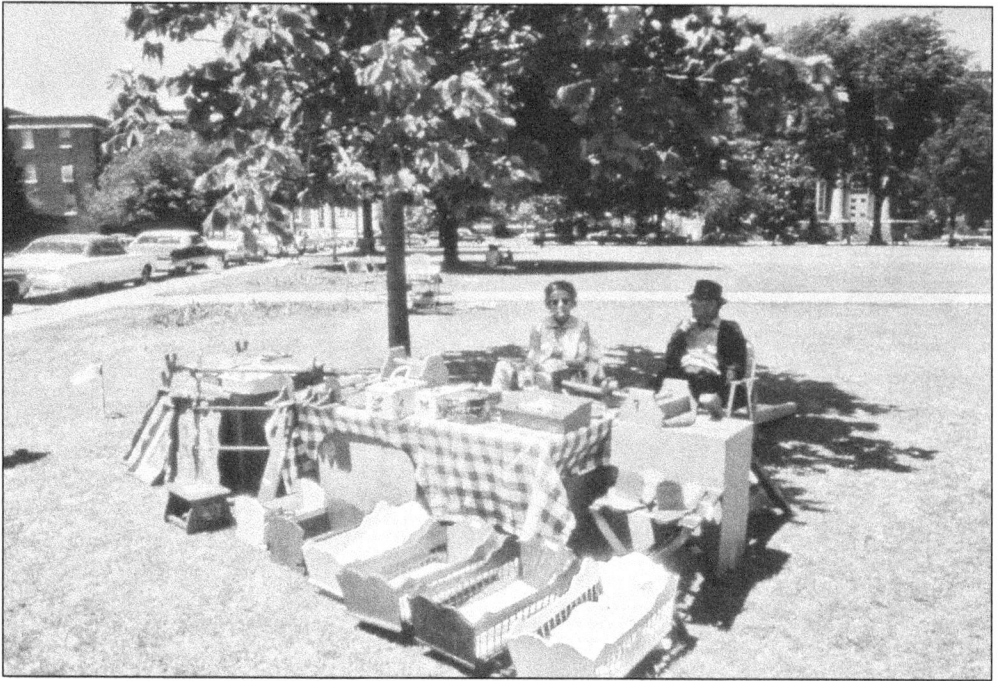

In the photograph above, any visitor who desires an old-fashioned wooden cradle for their baby—whether for a room decoration or for use—could often find it at the Arts and Crafts Festival in the 1970s. Below, a woodcarving artisan displays his various works—walled candlestick holders, flower boxes, and wood-canvassed depictions of art. (Both courtesy of Robert Wall.)

Above, at a booth at the bottom of the Provine Chapel, two women look at handmade candlesticks, chalice cups, and games of Chinese checkers and jump. Below, gourds hang from a netted display in a tree as an artisan sells ceramic cups to a visitor. Eventually, the festival became so popular that a second arts and crafts festival was formed for the spring. The spring festival began as the Dewitt Clinton Celebration in April 1984, but later became known as the Brick Street Festival, named because the event happens on redbricked Jefferson Street. (Both courtesy of Robert Wall.)

A bluegrass women's band performs in front of the Provine Chapel in the 1970s. (Courtesy of Robert Wall.)

Scores of Clinton children, most of whose parents moved to the city not more than 10 years before, listen to the live music in front of the Provine Chapel. (Courtesy of Robert Wall.)

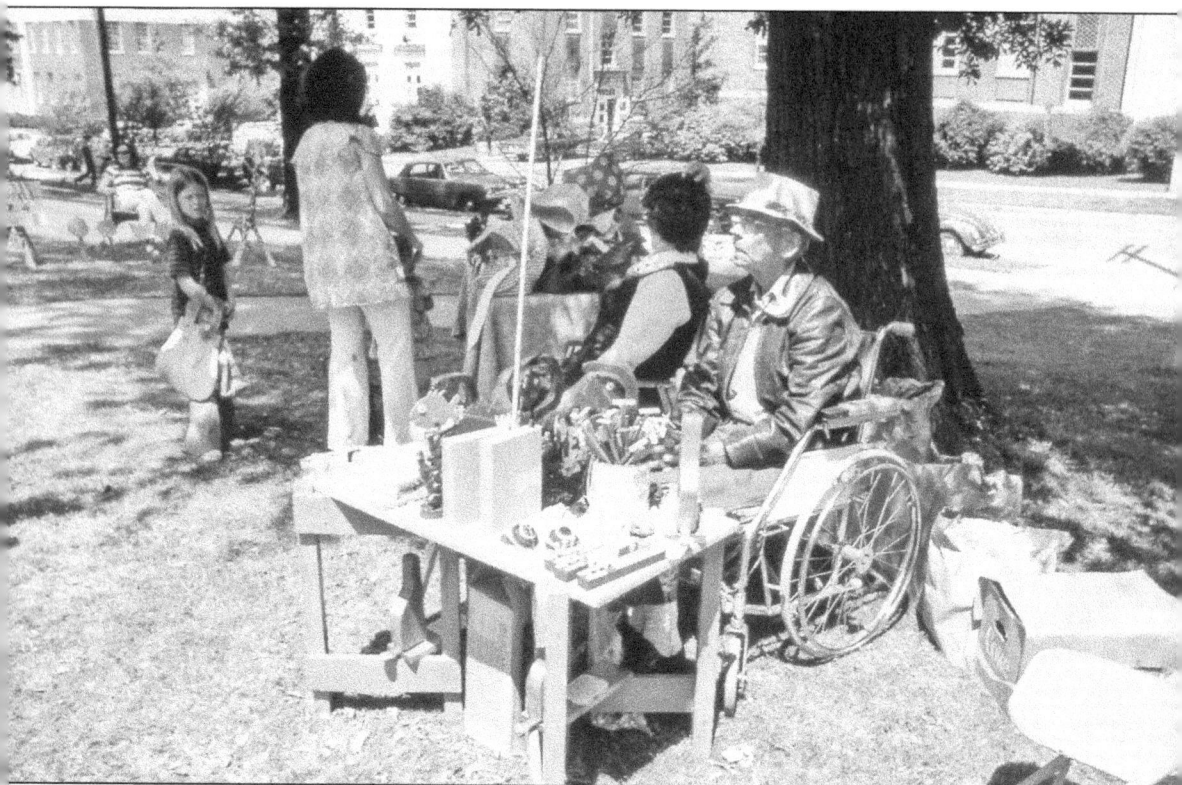

At a booth south of College Street, an old artisan in a wheelchair has handmade toys for sale for the children. (Courtesy of Robert Wall.)

Above, on the western side of the Provine Chapel, a couple views an artisan's works that are invisible to the camera's lens. Behind them is a virtual garden of art and canvass. Below, more art is on display at the Arts and Crafts Festival. (Both courtesy of Robert Wall.)

The Clinton High School Arrows Marching Band (above) marches past the Mississippi College tennis courts during the homecoming parade in 1976. Each school in the Clinton public school system usually participates in the parade. Below, each high school club and class prepares its own float for the parade. (Both courtesy of Robert Wall.)

This caterpillar float, one of the longest of any Clinton parade, was propelled down College Street by CHS girl power during a Clinton Homecoming Parade. (Courtesy of Robert Wall.)

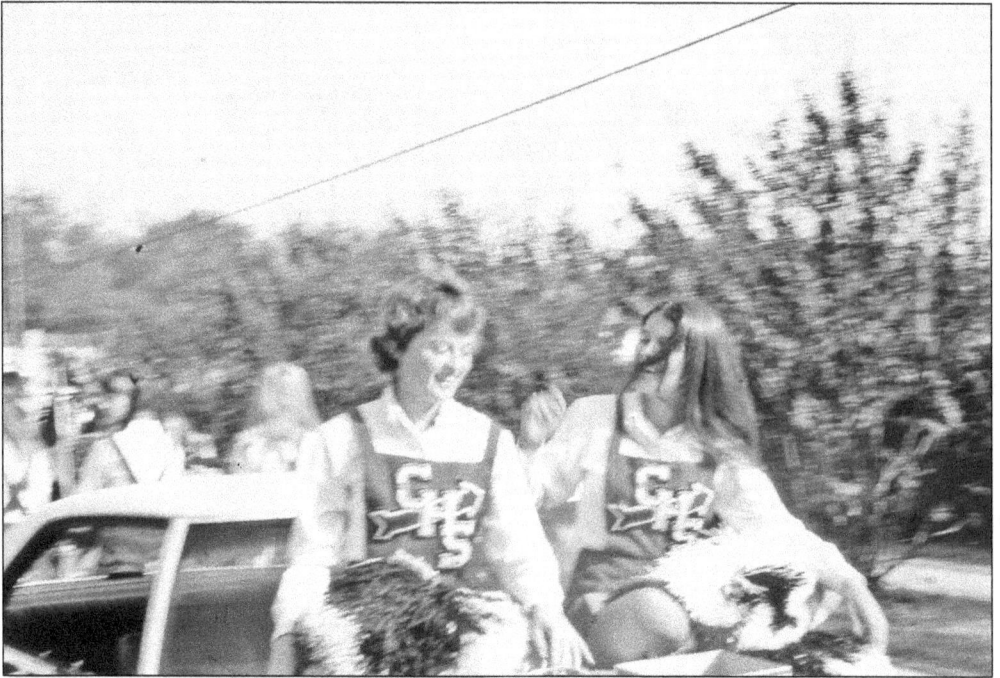

In the picture above, Clinton High School (CHS) cheerleaders ride toward the old Robinson Field with the old Ratliff Motor Company blurry in the background. Clinton Junior High School (CJHS) cheerleaders (below) cruise down College Street on the hood of a vintage Chevy Nova during the CHS Homecoming Parade. (Both courtesy of Robert Wall.)

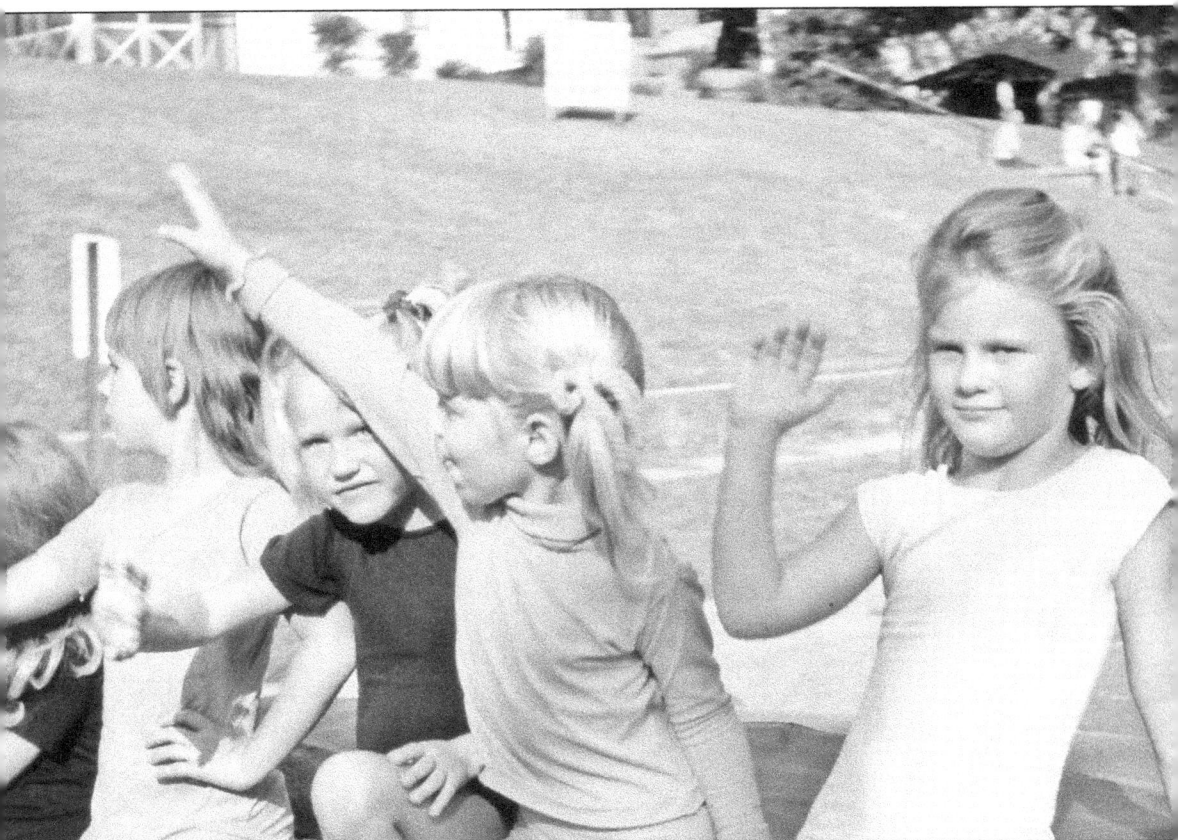

Children ride in the back of one of several convertible cars provided for the homecoming parades. (Courtesy of Robert Wall.)

Children baton throwers precede the high school Arrows Band after they have passed the old Ratliff Motor Company and are marching by the practice tennis courts at Robinson Field. (Courtesy of Robert Wall.)

Above is a closer view of one of the young baton throwers. In the photograph below, a member of the Clinton Band Color Guard precedes the band. (Both courtesy of Robert Wall.)

The U.S. Bicentennial celebration on July 4, 1976, began in Clinton with the ringing of the MC chapel bell at noon. The festivities were centered in Olde Towne on Clinton's historic redbrick streets. (Courtesy of Robert Wall.)

A lady in her yellow Sunday dress greets a young family on the streets of Olde Towne Clinton during the U.S. Bicentennial celebration in 1976. (Courtesy of Robert Wall.)

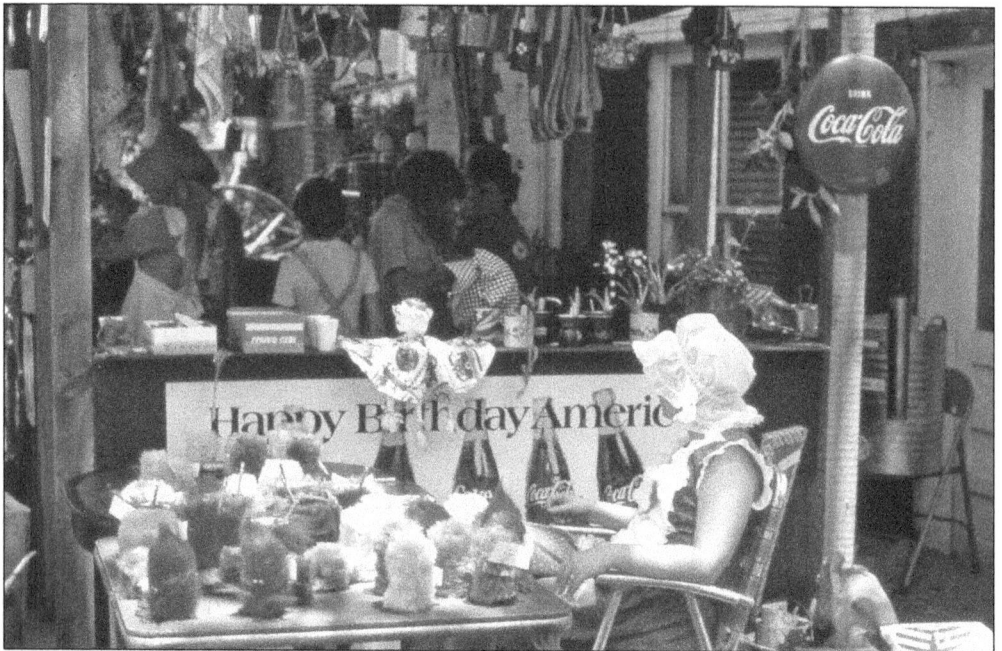

In the photograph above, a woman in Revolutionary costume sells a beverage in an odd, furry cup. Below, two women in their 1776 dresses walk on the sidewalk along West Leake Street on their way to Olde Towne for the U.S. Bicentennial festivities. (Both courtesy of Robert Wall.)

A woman across the street from city hall buys a loaf of homemade bread from one of the vendors at the U.S. Bicentennial celebration. Behind her, the bricks that makeup Jefferson Street are clearly visible. In 1929, an African American man was hired by the city to lay about 614,000 red bricks on Jefferson, West Leake, New Prospect, and Monroe Streets. The bricks cost the city $460.95 and $463.57 for the labor. Today Monroe and New Prospect Streets have been paved over, but Jefferson and West Leake Streets remain a Clinton showpiece and a wonderful gathering place for Clinton's two arts and crafts festivals, as well as other civic events. (Courtesy of Robert Wall.)

A mother in Revolutionary costume and her two sons, one a member of Boy Scouts of America, watch the U.S. Bicentennial events near city hall. (Courtesy of Robert Wall.)

In the photograph above, some Clintonians are lucky enough to ride in a horse-drawn wagon on the brick streets, similarly to how the founding fathers would have ridden on the bricked streets of Philadelphia, Pennsylvania. Below, two women on a warm Independence Day walk north on Jefferson Street wearing their long dresses. (Both courtesy of Robert Wall.)

A boy in a Revolutionary-era hat guides a girl on a horse south on Jefferson Street. The man to the boy's right, with his leather canteen for water, reminds us that Clinton in 1776 was frontier country. (Courtesy of Robert Wall.)

Mississippi College Bible professor Charles Wilson and Mary Jane Whitfield are photographed walking down Jefferson Street by photographer Robert Wall, who is standing north at the intersection of West Leake and Jefferson Streets. (Courtesy of Robert Wall.)

In the photograph above, Mary Jane Whitfield, wearing a Revolutionary-era dress and holding her bonnet, and other Clintonians await the next event near the stage just south of city hall. Below, a mixture of Revolutionary costumes and modern clothes clash in the middle of Olde Towne. (Both courtesy of Robert Wall.)

Charles Wilson, Mary Jane Whitfield, and Judy Brewer visit near the intersection of Jefferson and West Leake Streets in front of Western Auto. (Courtesy of Robert Wall.)

In the photograph above, a young couple pushes their baby over Olde Towne's brick streets in a fancy stroller. Below, the old Western Auto once housed the Bank of Clinton, and in the late 1990s, it housed Gravity Coffee House. (Both courtesy of Robert Wall.)

The Mississippi National Guard marches down College Street during one of Clinton's first Christmas parades. Charles Blass, Clinton's mayor from 1969 to 1981, had a daughter named Charlene who opened a baton school in the city, and she used her influence to urge her father to begin an annual Christmas parade in 1973. (Courtesy of Robert Wall.)

In the late 1970s, Clinton's Eastside Elementary School had a beginner band for musically astute children and took great pride in showing off the marching skills of the future of the Clinton High School Arrows Band. (Courtesy of Robert Wall.)

In the photograph above, the Mississippi College Choctaw Band marches down College Street toward campus. Below, the Clinton High School Color Guard marches before the Arrows Band carrying drill rifles. (Both courtesy of Robert Wall.)

Above, the Mississippi College Color Guard marches in the 1976 Christmas parade. Below, the school of dance uses its float to showcase its students' ballet skills. In the Clinton Christmas parade, each float is judged for a prize. (Both courtesy of Robert Wall.)

On his paramount float in the 1976 Christmas parade, Santa Claus has two helpers in candy cane–striped outfits. (Courtesy of Robert Wall.)

The Indian Guides was an organization for children interested in going into the Boy Scouts of America when they became older. (Courtesy of Robert Wall.)

The Indian Guides was a popular local organization for Clinton youths, which is why they sometimes had more than one float in the Christmas parade. (Courtesy of Robert Wall.)

If a Clinton group or organization did not have much money for a float, sometimes a little ingenuity did the trick. (Courtesy of Robert Wall.)

In the photograph above, a host of angels adorns what is probably the float for one of Clinton's multiple church groups. Below is a closer picture of one of the little angels. (Both courtesy of Robert Wall.)

Another church float portrays a living, breathing Nativity scene. Since the 1960s, the number of churches in Clinton multiplied almost as fast as its population. (Courtesy of Robert Wall.)

In the above photograph, a float starts out from Morrison Heights Baptist Church to make its several-block journey to the Mississippi College tennis courts, which is the route the parade has taken for the past 30 years. Below, a *Sesame Street*–theme float was a favorite among the children. (Both courtesy of Robert Wall.)

This aerial photograph shows Clinton from the northern side of the city. Mississippi College is visible from the upper-right corner of the picture before the construction of the coliseum. (Courtesy of MC.)

This aerial photograph shows Mississippi College from the south side of the campus. Interstate 20 cuts across the middle of the photograph and shows the undeveloped land south of the interstate, which was college property and is MCI-WorldCom in 2008. In the 1980s, Robinson Cemetery was discovered in those woods, which was the resting place of Col. Raymond Robinson and his son-in-law Judge Isaac Caldwell, the man who fought to make Clinton the state capital of Mississippi and was killed on the dueling fields just off of Clinton-Raymond Road. The discovery of the cemetery caused a conflict between preservationists and college president Lewis Nobles, who wanted to develop the land. Eventually, the cemetery was moved to the Clinton Cemetery. (Courtesy of MC.)

In the 1970s, the City of Clinton began to annex more land to the east toward Jackson and to the west in the open county. Two areas that Clinton annexed in western Hinds County were Lovett and Sumner Hill, both areas located around Northside Drive and named for nearby county schools. Today Lovett serves as an elementary school for sixth-grade children, while Sumner Hill serves as a ninth-grade high school. (Courtesy of Robert Wall.)

When Clinton began to annex properties in Hinds County, the city had to deal with the many businesses, schools, churches, and communities that already existed. The county schools were absorbed into the Clinton Public School District, and businesses such as this three-pump station continued much as it had. However, businesses of a more questionable legality—"razor joints" as then councilman Walter Howell put it—were incompatible with Clinton's image as a small, Southern Baptist suburb and college town, and these had to leave or move back across the new city line. (Courtesy of Robert Wall.)

Clinton developer Maurice King built this home in the 1970s, which is modeled closely after the historical Dunleith bed and breakfast in Natchez, Mississippi. King today lives in the Heights, a neighborhood he developed. (Courtesy of Robert Wall.)

The Pleasant Green Baptist Church on College Street is one of the oldest continuing African American Baptist churches in Clinton. Until the Civil War, many African slaves attended church with their white masters. However, after emancipation, most Africans chose to leave the white churches and create their own church communities. (Courtesy of Robert Wall.)

In the late 1980s, Vice Pres. George H. W. Bush came to Clinton to visit Mississippi College, the Mississippi College School of Law in Jackson, and to visit the students and teachers at Clinton High School. Bush is seen walking past the doors of what was then the Clinton High School auditorium. The third man to the left of Vice President Bush is Dr. Sam Bounds, then principal of Clinton High School, who later left to become superintendent of the Brookhaven schools and who serves as executive director of Mississippi Schools Superintendents Association in 2008. (Courtesy of the Clinton Visitor Center.)

You are invited to a private reception for

Ronald Reagan

Monday, April 28, 1975, 4:00-4:30 p.m.

in the home of President Nobles.

Please bring this invitation with you.

Casual dress

Ronald Reagan

On April 28, 1975, former California governor Ronald Reagan visited with around 100 students and faculty at the home of then Mississippi College president Dr. Lewis Nobles. Reagan was preparing himself for his unsuccessful campaign to win the Republican nomination over incumbent president Gerald Ford. Since the 1960s, Clinton was one of the fastest-growing communities in the South, and Mississippi politicians often came to court its conservative middle-class voters. However, with the arrival of Reagan in 1975 and Jimmy Carter at the Clinton home, the Cedars, in 1976, this courtship became national. (Courtesy of MC.)

Clinton mayor-elect Walter Howell (right) and Mississippi's U.S. senator Thad Cochran meet after a political address on the Mississippi College campus in 1981. Mayor Howell, as a MC history professor, had been the director of the college's American Studies Seminar, and Senator Cochran had been his guest ever since his election to the U.S. Senate in 1978. (Courtesy of Walter Howell.)

BIBLIOGRAPHY

Aikens, Nolan, Alice Hobson, Jan Hurt, and John Murphy. "Clinton—History and Progress: A Curriculum Unit for Middle-School Social Studies." Clinton, MS: unpublished. 1992–1993.

American Association of University Women, Clinton-Raymond branch. *Down Brick Streets: A Guide to Historical Sites in Clinton, Mississippi.* AAUW, 1976.

Ashcraft, Carey E. "Country Boy Infantry: 'The Blue Devils,' 88th Infantry Division: 1944–1945." Self-published. 1996.

Brough, Charles Hillman. "Historic Clinton." *Publications of the Mississippi Historical Society,* vol. 7 (1903): 281–316.

Cardin, Tommy, Lydia Jones, Paul Mucho, and Ed Smith. "Restoration of the Sarah Dickey Grave Site: 1995/96 Leadership Clinton Team Project Report." Unpublished, 1995–1996.

Faucette, Shirley. "Clinton Yesterday." *Journal of Mississippi History* XL.1 (1978).

Gough, Norman. "Mississippi College Historical Spots." Unpublished, c. 1995.

Howell, Walter. Personal interview. 13 October 2007.

———. "Report from City Hall: Theatre Production Will Afford a Special Treat." *The Clinton News.* 2 February 1984.

Martin, Charles E. "Clinton: The Athens of Mississippi." Friends of the Clinton Library. A. E. Wood Memorial Library, Clinton, MS: unpublished lecture. 2 Sept. 1999.

———. "Mississippi College: From a Frontier Academy to Modern University." *The Clinton News.* 6 January 2000.

———. "The Navy V12 Unit at Mississippi College." Unpublished. 2000.

McDonald, Ed. Personal interview. 29 September 2007.

McIntire, Carl. "Mt. Salus Presbyterian Church Anniversary Set." *The Clarion Ledger.* 28 Feb. 1982: 4G.

Skates, John Ray. "German Prisoners of War in Mississippi, 1943–1946." *Mississippi History Now* (2001). Mississippi Historical Society, mshistory.k12.ms.us/features/feature20/germanprisonersofwar.html. Sept. 2001.

Visit us at
arcadiapublishing.com

www.ingramcontent.com/pod-product-compliance
Lightning Source LLC
Chambersburg PA
CBHW080614110426
42813CB00006B/1499